Have You Seen a Kangaroo?

When You Go to Kindergarten

R SNOWMAN

You Can Do Amazing Things

I am Beautiful and Brave

I Will Always Love You

ook at Me!

r̶t to the World

MY LOVE WILL STAY FOREVER

If My Love Were a Season

When You Go to Kindergarten

Mom, Look at Me!

HELLO MOON!

When you read a book
in your cozy nook,
you do something great.

You celebrate the joy
that no one can destroy.

A book is a friend
with whom you like to spend
hour after hour,

until the moon gets pink and blue,
and your bond feels true.

A book opens a door
that you've never thought of before.

You Are Wonderful

a door to a new adventure
where you search for treasure,
magic, wonder, and pleasure.

You are a brave explorer
ready to discover
magical places
with new cultures
and beautiful faces.

The world is yours.

There are no closed doors.

You are a keen traveler
crossing border after border,
looking for joy and meaning,
wisdom and dreaming.

For a curious spirit like yours,
anything is possible, of course.

You can touch the stars
and fly beyond Mars.

You can tame wild creatures
and paint them in cute pictures.

You can go through ugly storms
and still hold the sun in your arms.

You can do amazing things
when books are your passion.

A great book lights up
your mind and heart

You Are a Gift to the World

till there is no dark part.

A book is a ray of light,
and so is your heart.

Dear child,
you can do amazing things.

Now, just go
and find a good book.

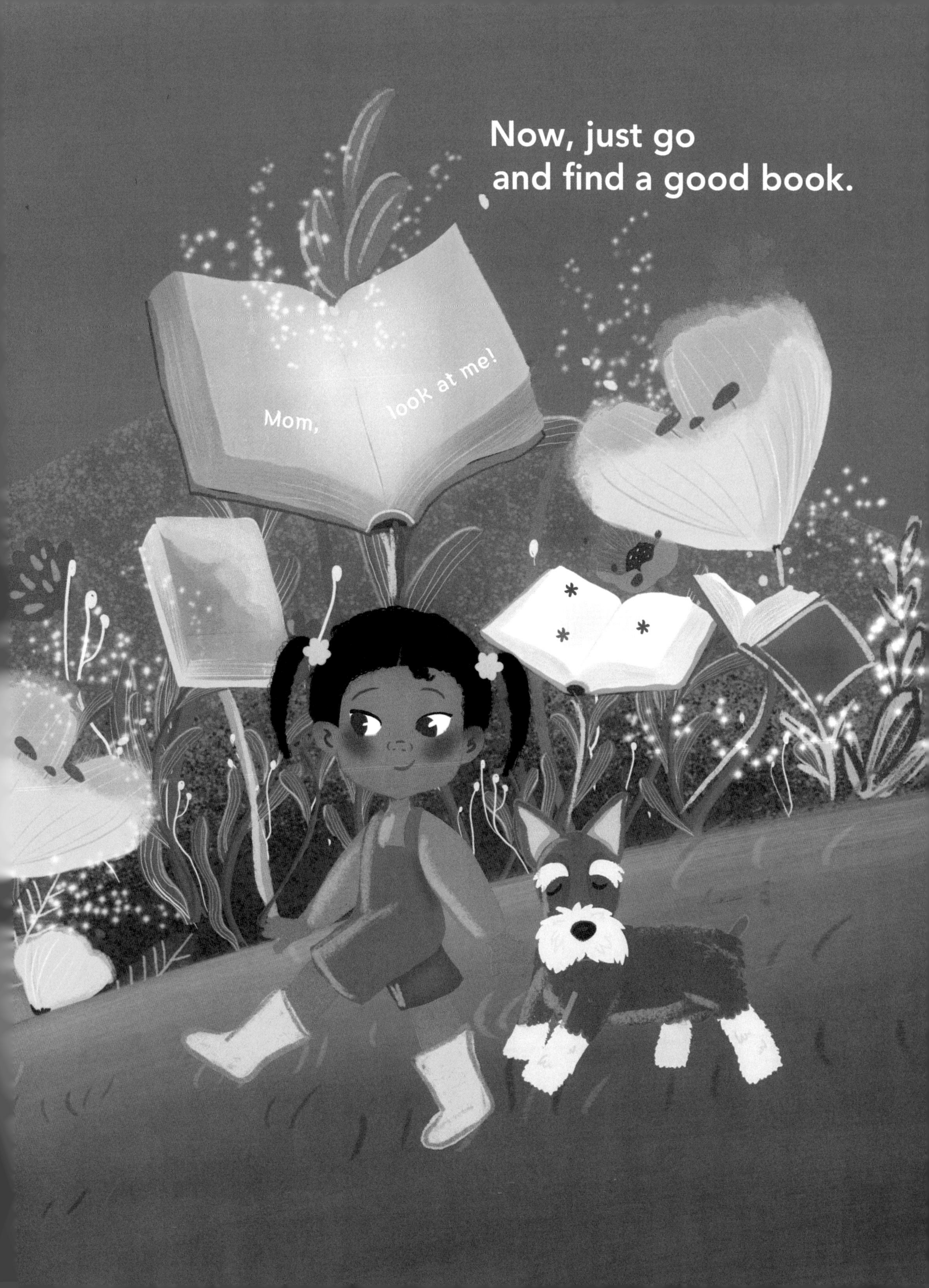

Then, spread the joy

with all your might,

for the world needs you
and your light.

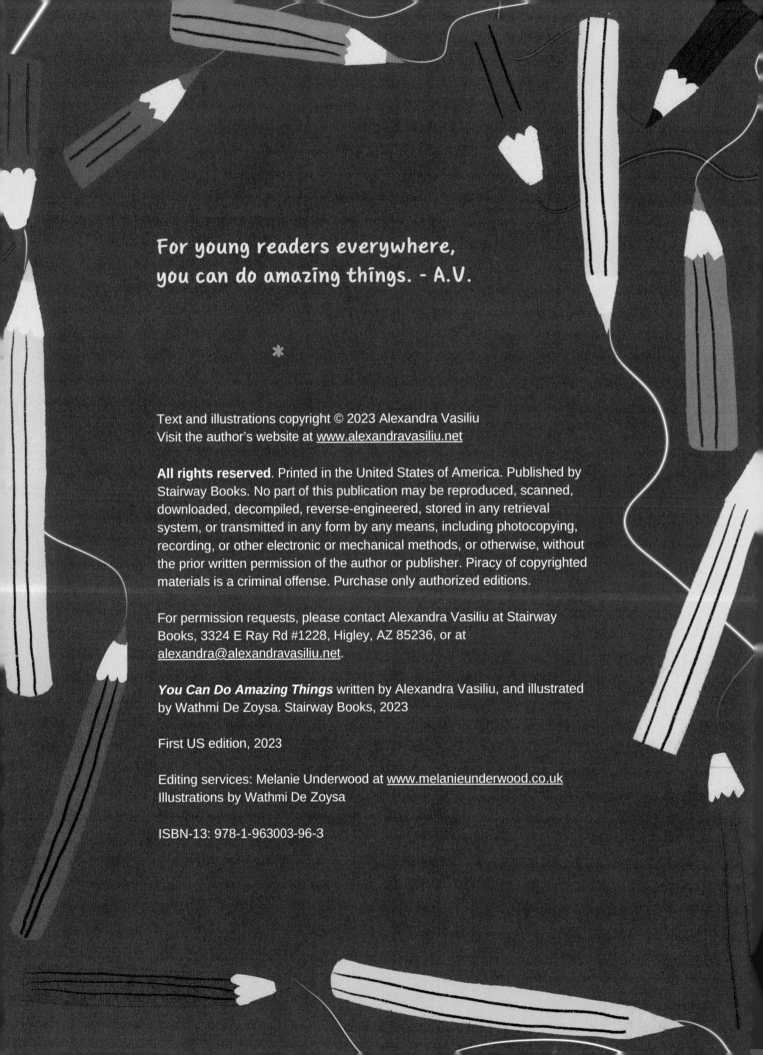

For young readers everywhere,
you can do amazing things. - A.V.

*

For permission requests, please contact Alexandra Vasiliu at Stairway Books, 3324 E Ray Rd #1228, Higley, AZ 85236, or at alexandra@alexandravasiliu.net.

You Can Do Amazing Things written by Alexandra Vasiliu, and illustrated by Wathmi De Zoysa. Stairway Books, 2023

First US edition, 2023

Editing services: Melanie Underwood at www.melanieunderwood.co.uk
Illustrations by Wathmi De Zoysa

ISBN-13: 978-1-963003-96-3

Made in the USA
Las Vegas, NV
20 December 2023

83237045R00021